MW01399625

THIS COLORING BOOK

BELONGS TO:

____

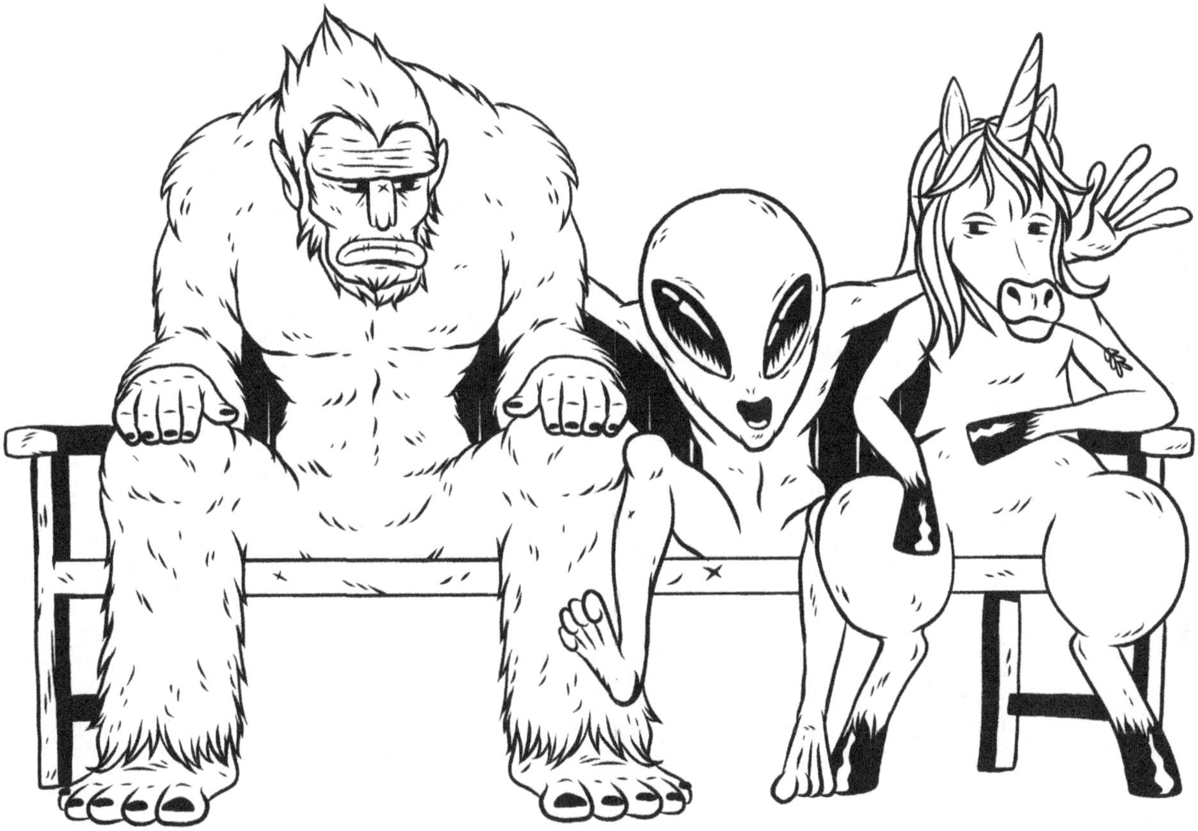

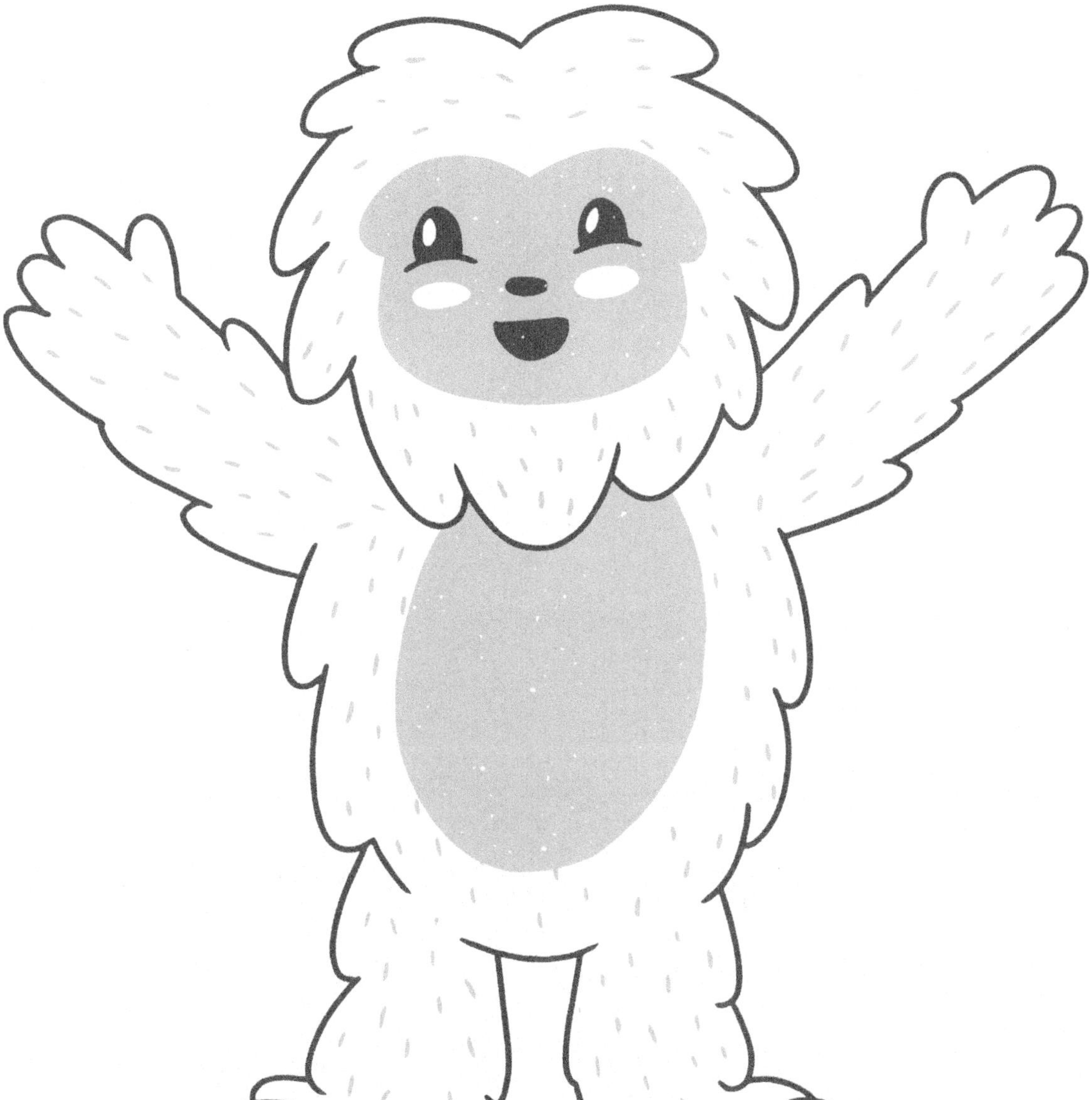

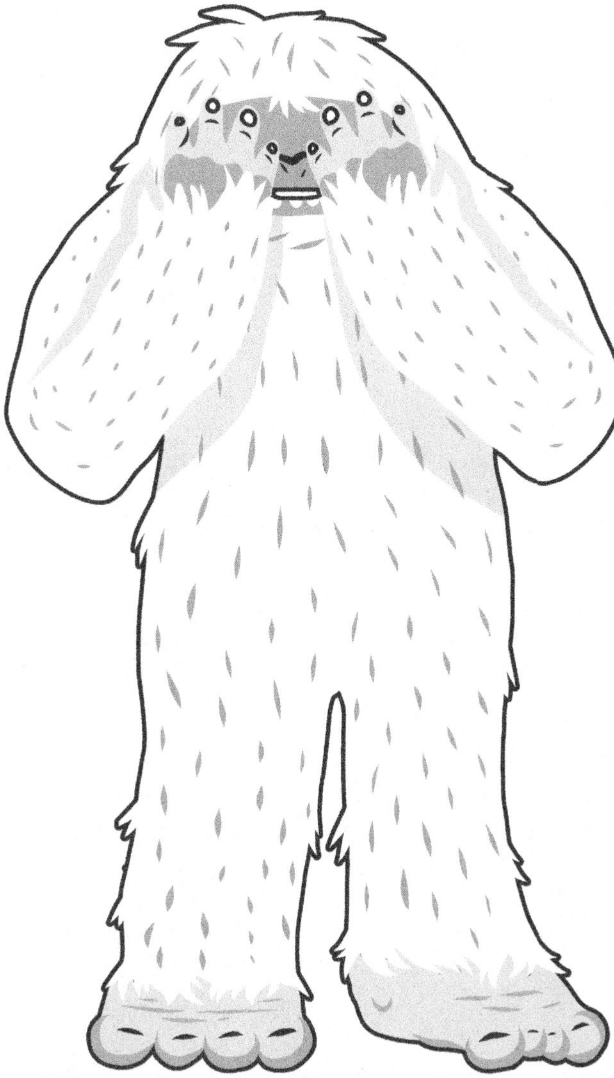

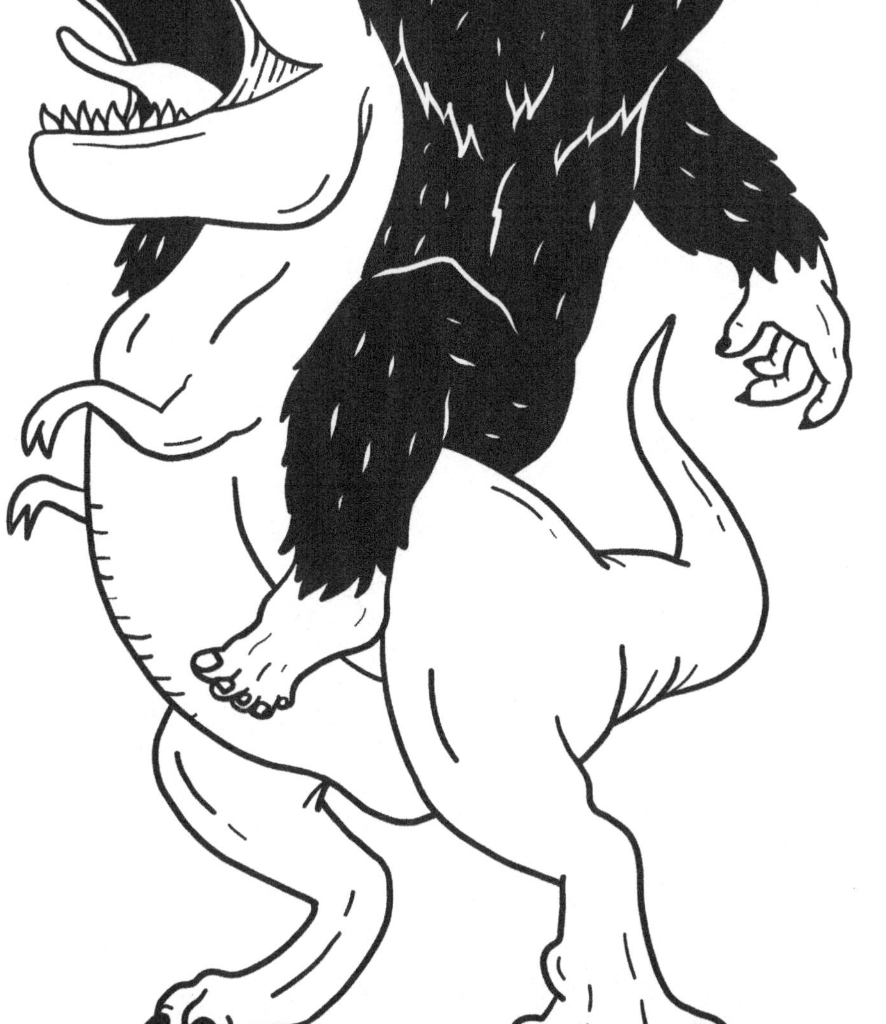

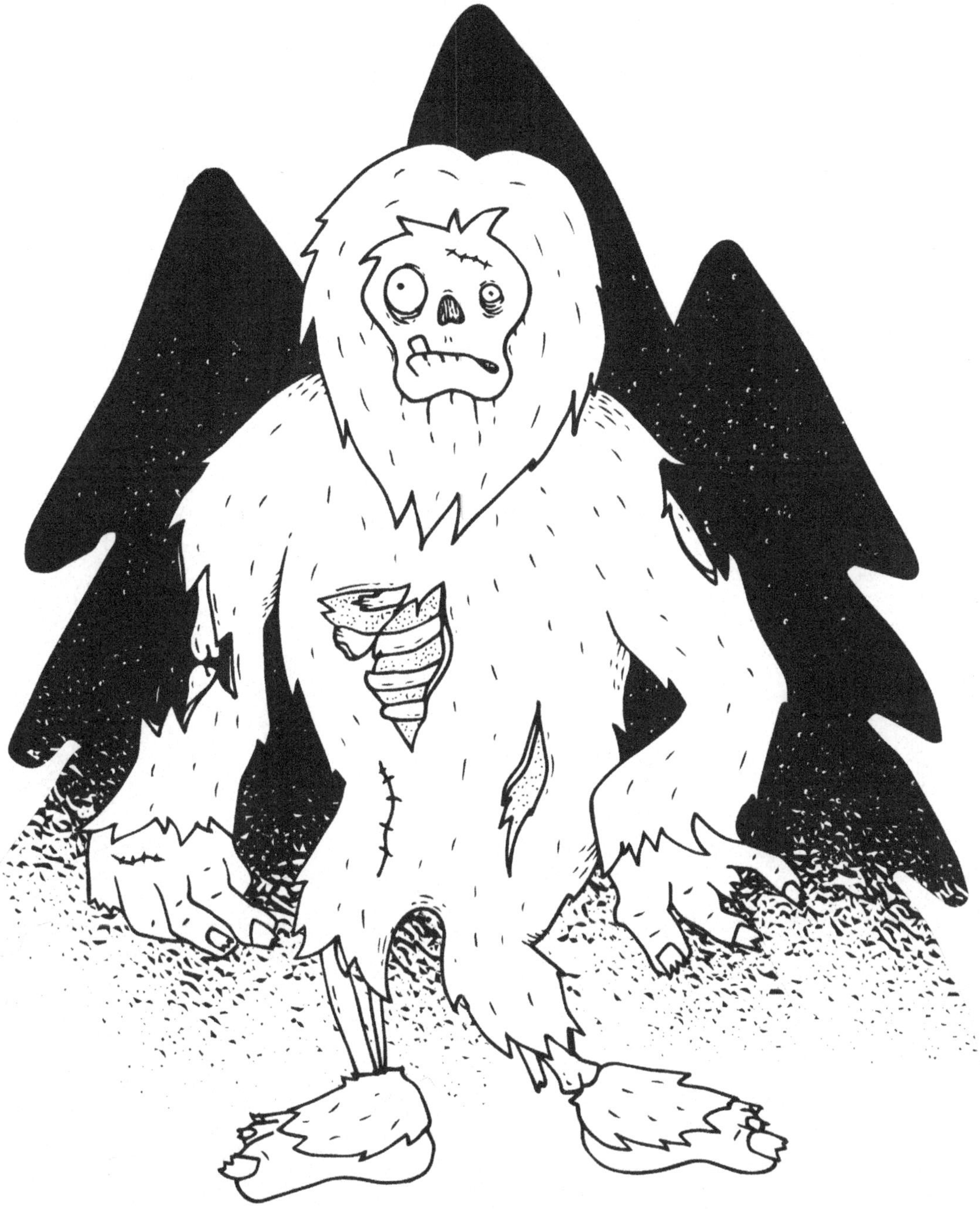

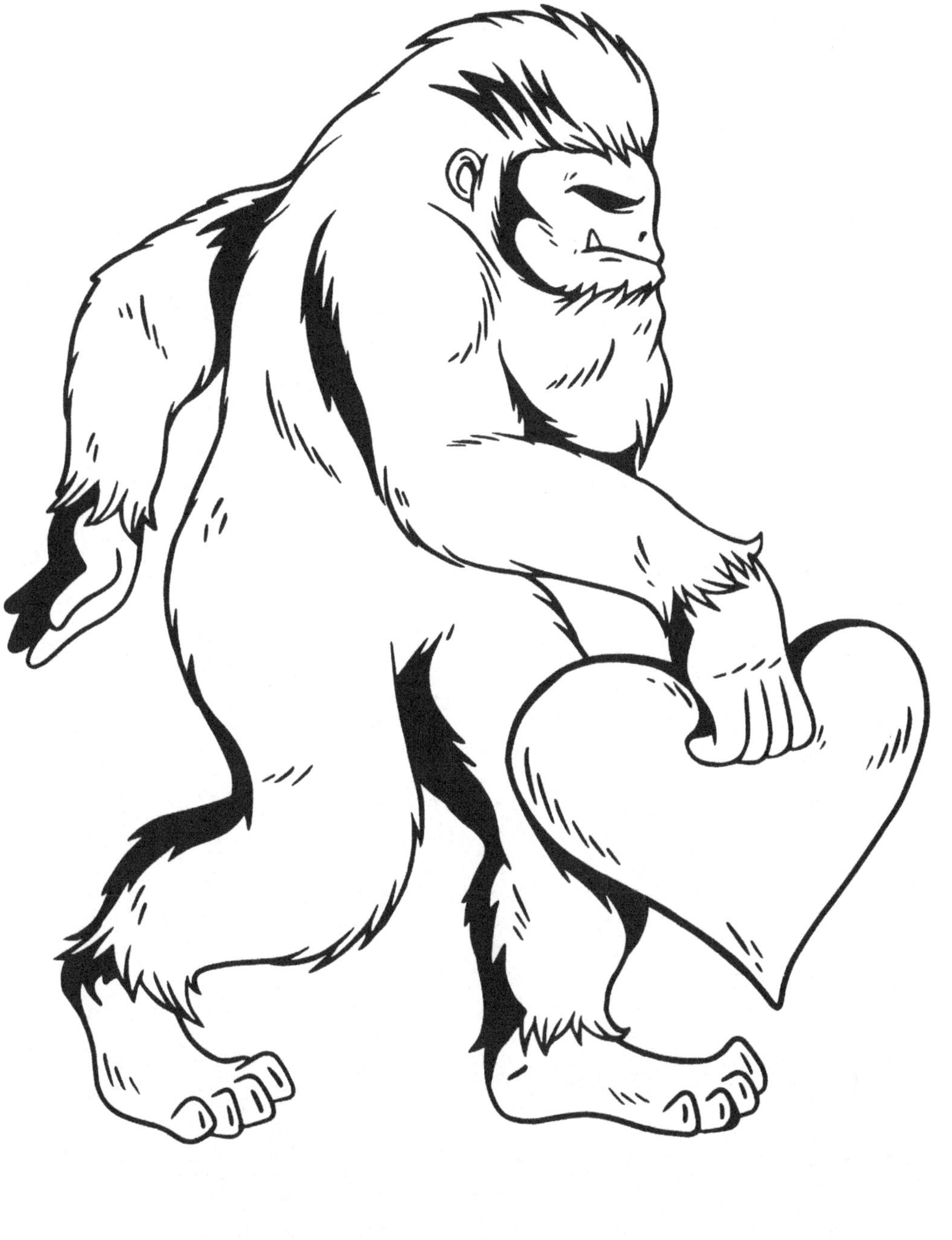

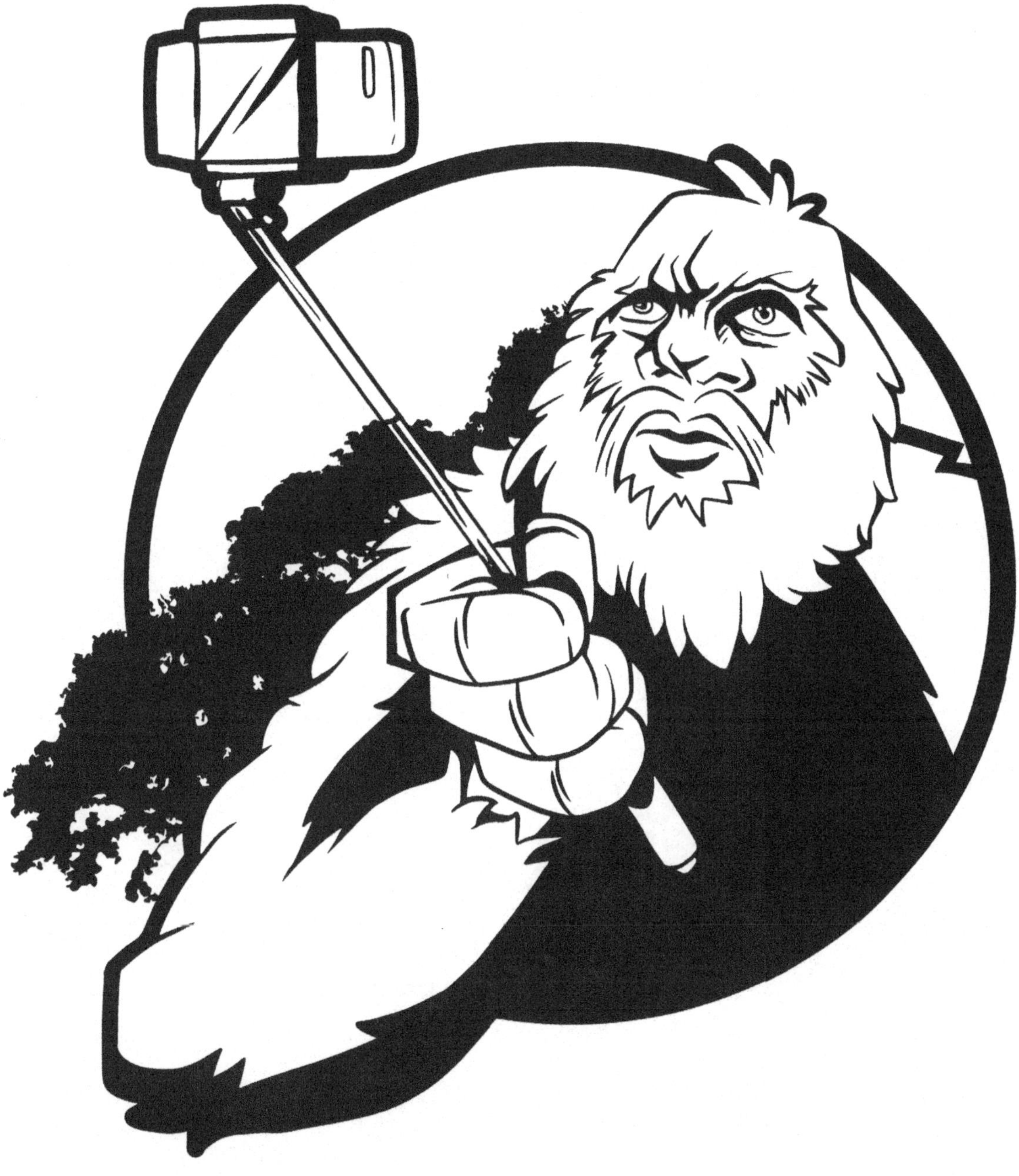

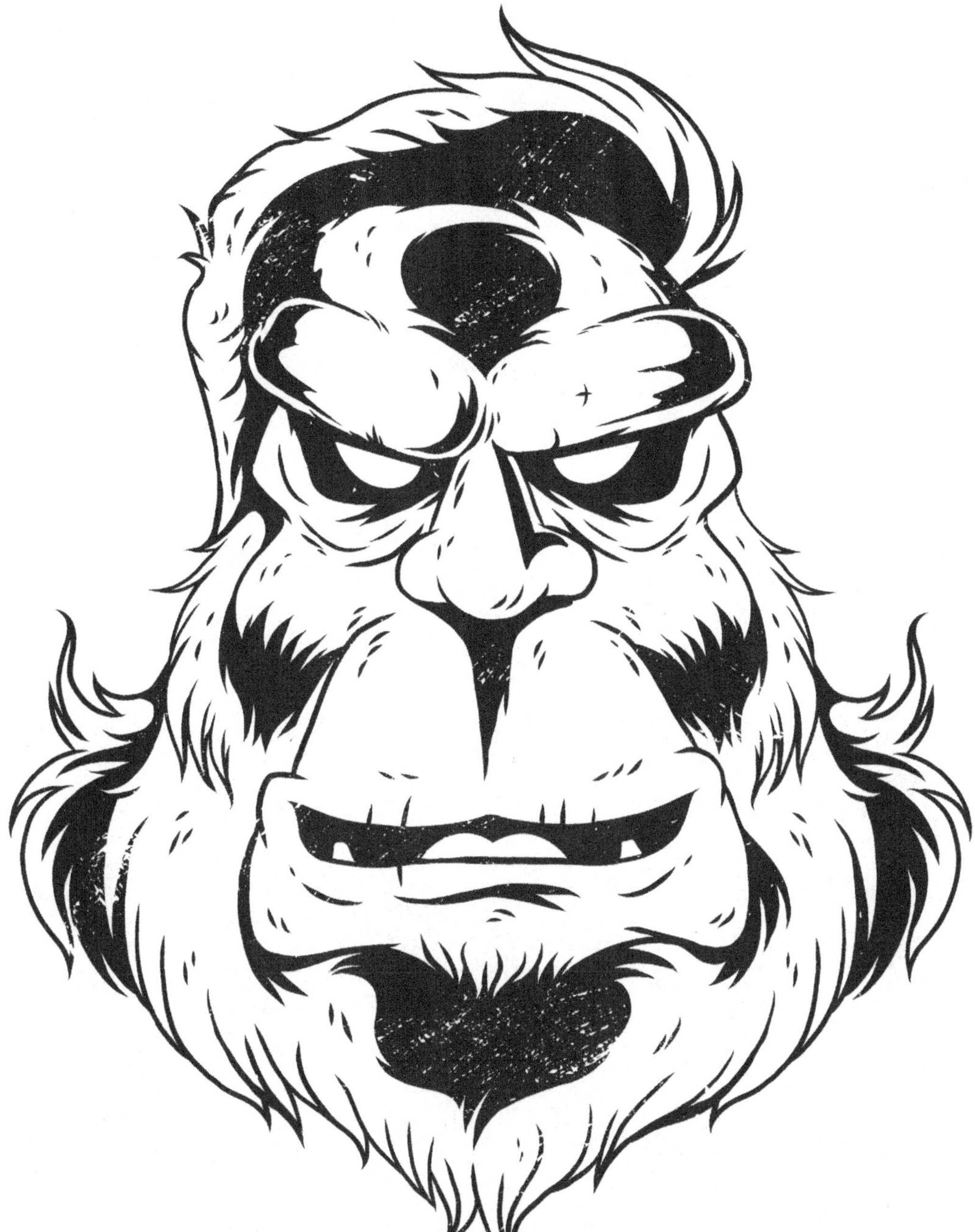

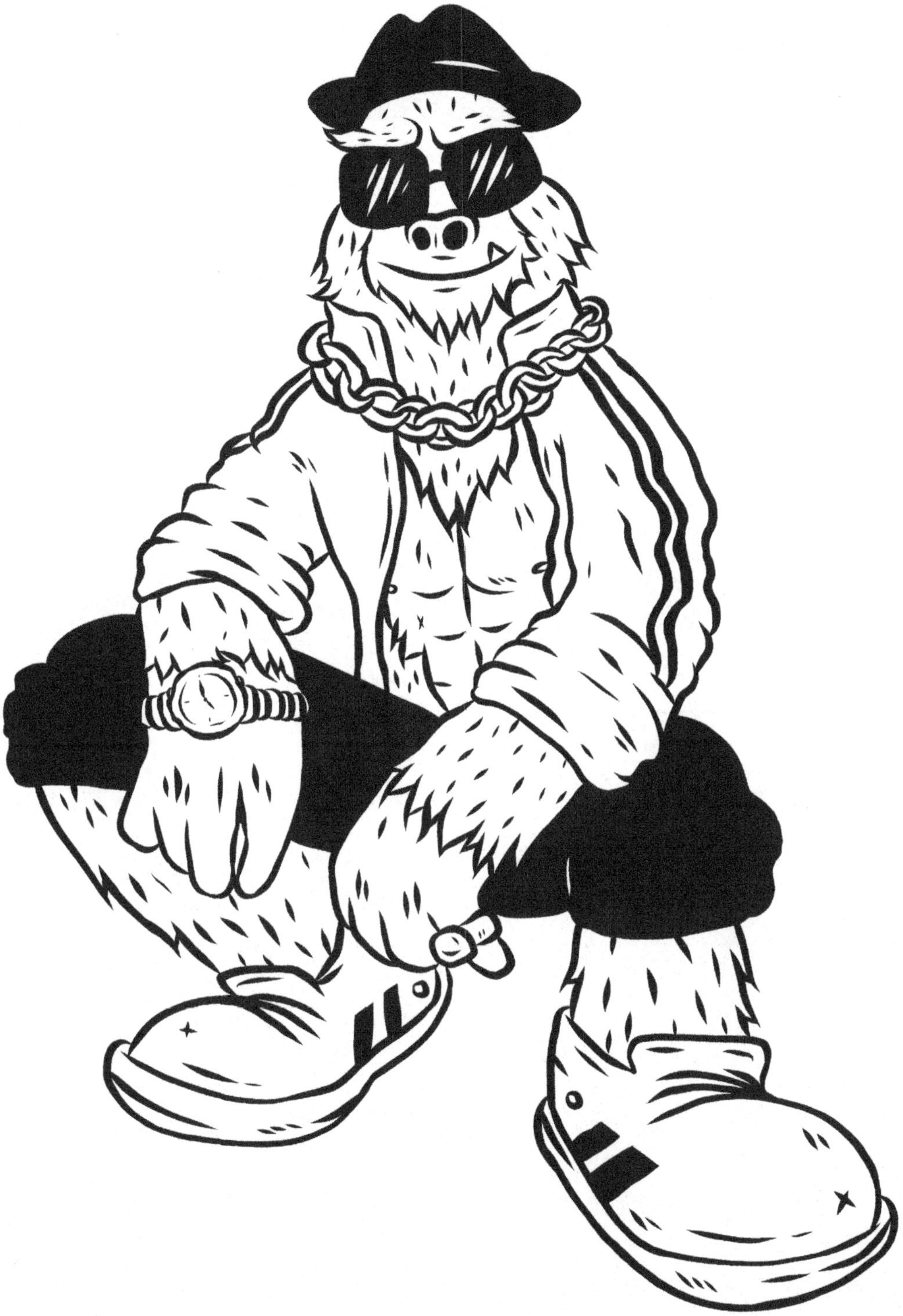

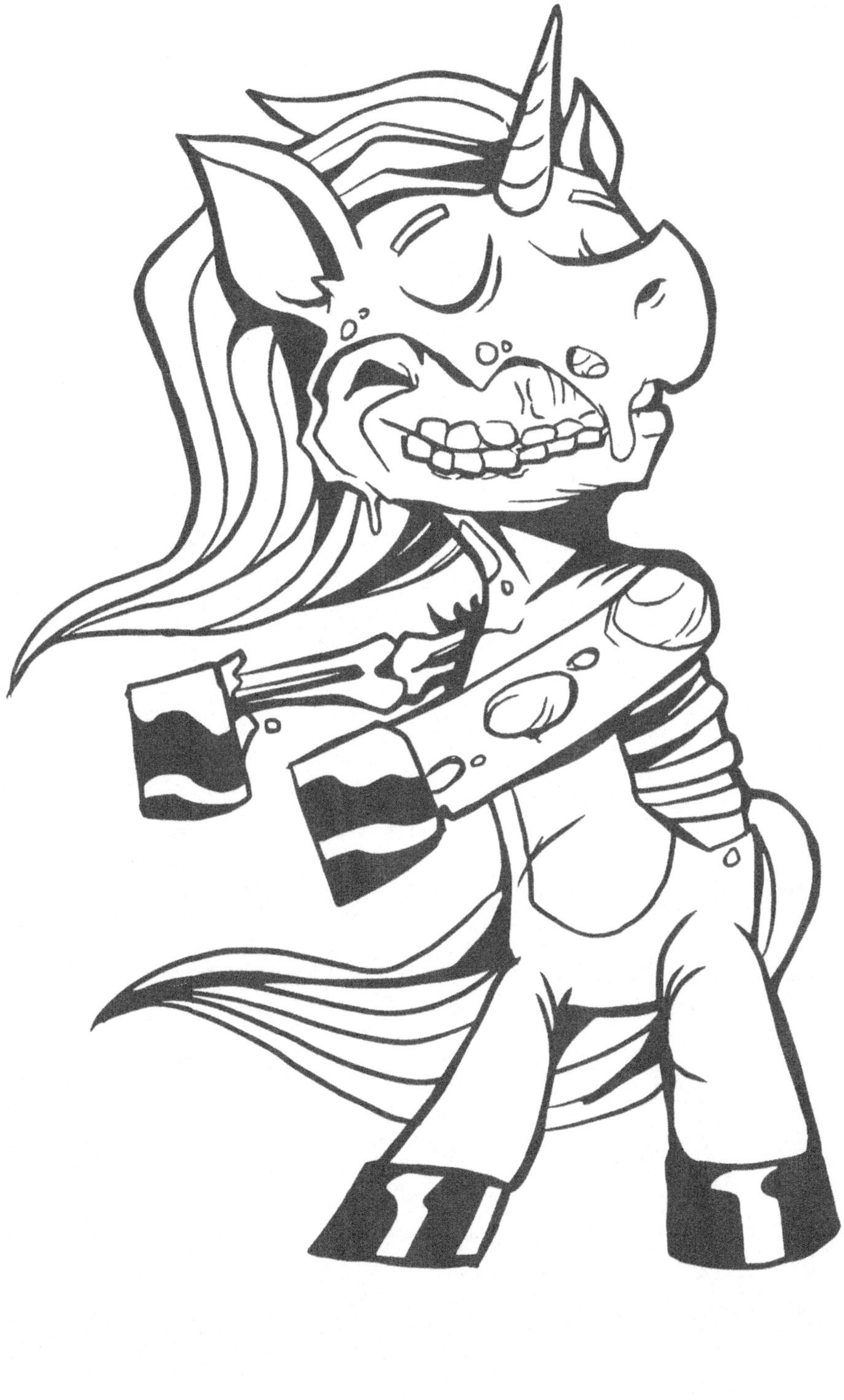

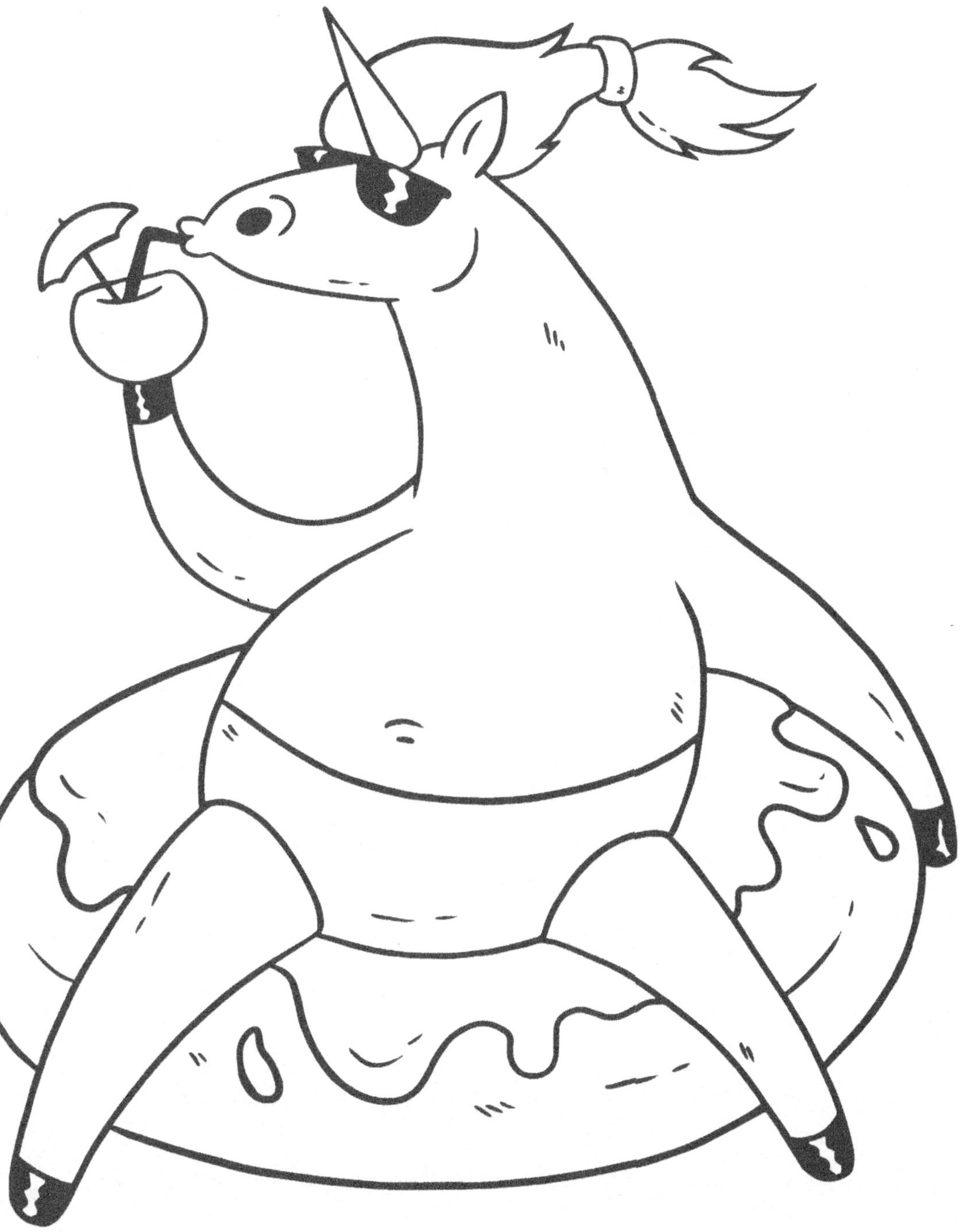

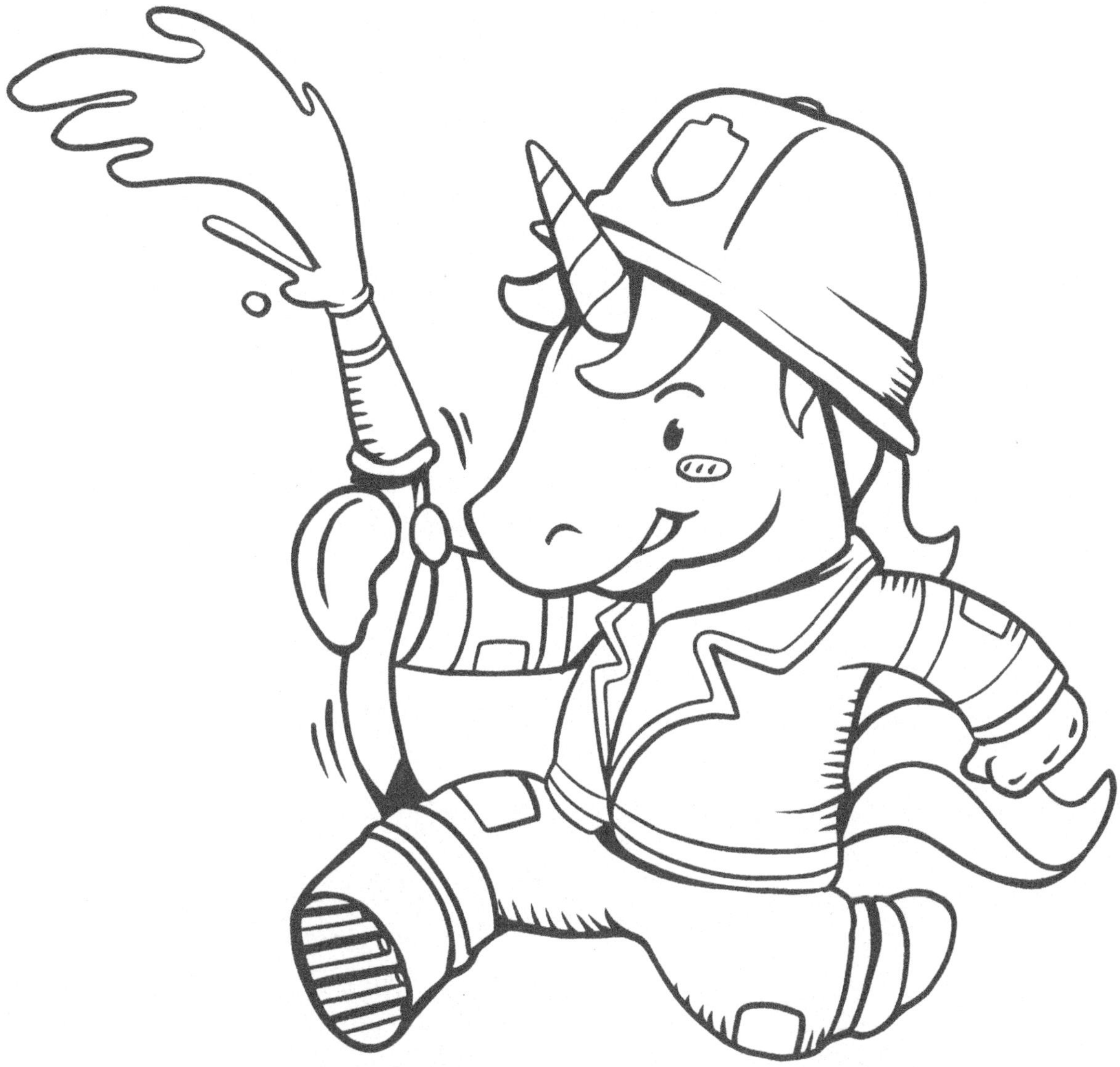

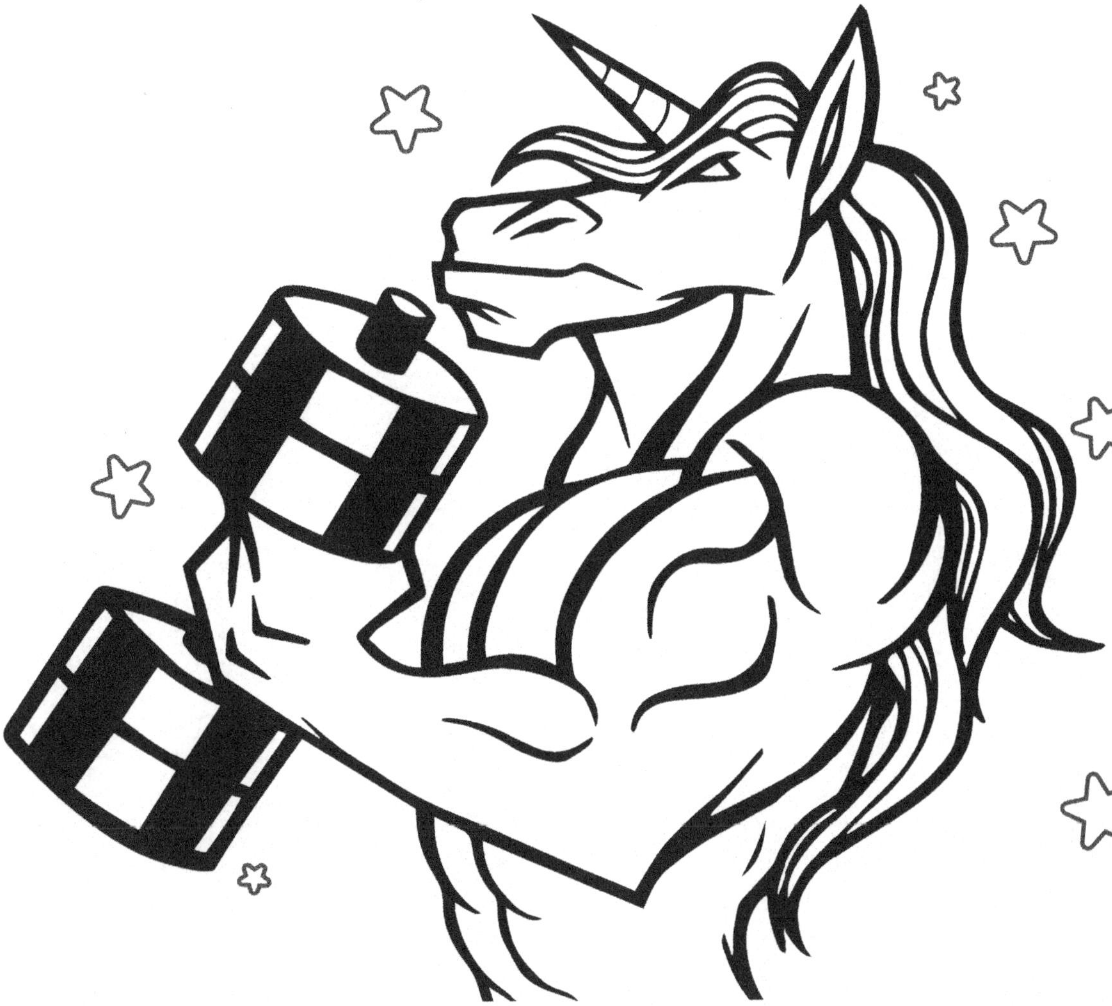

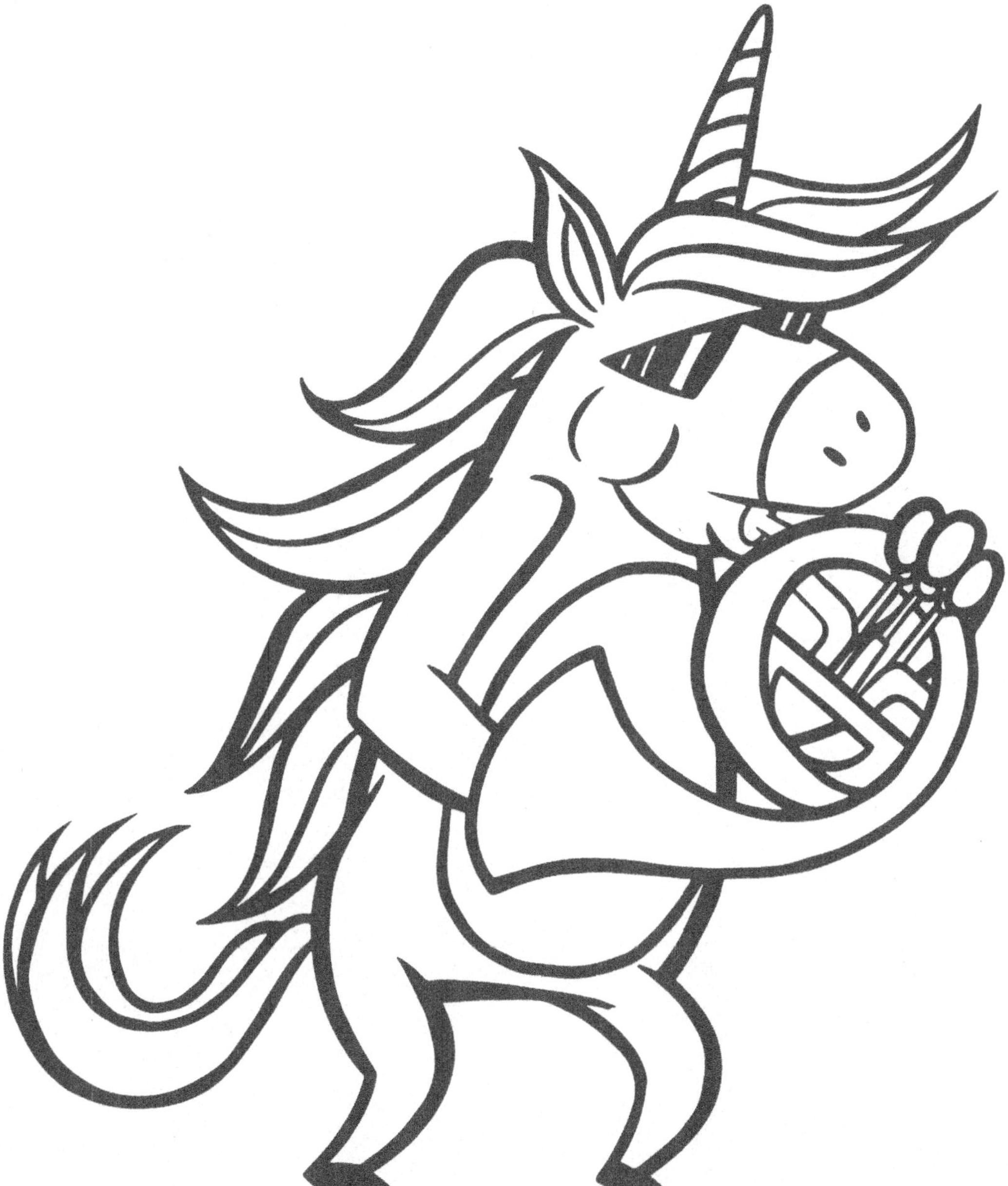

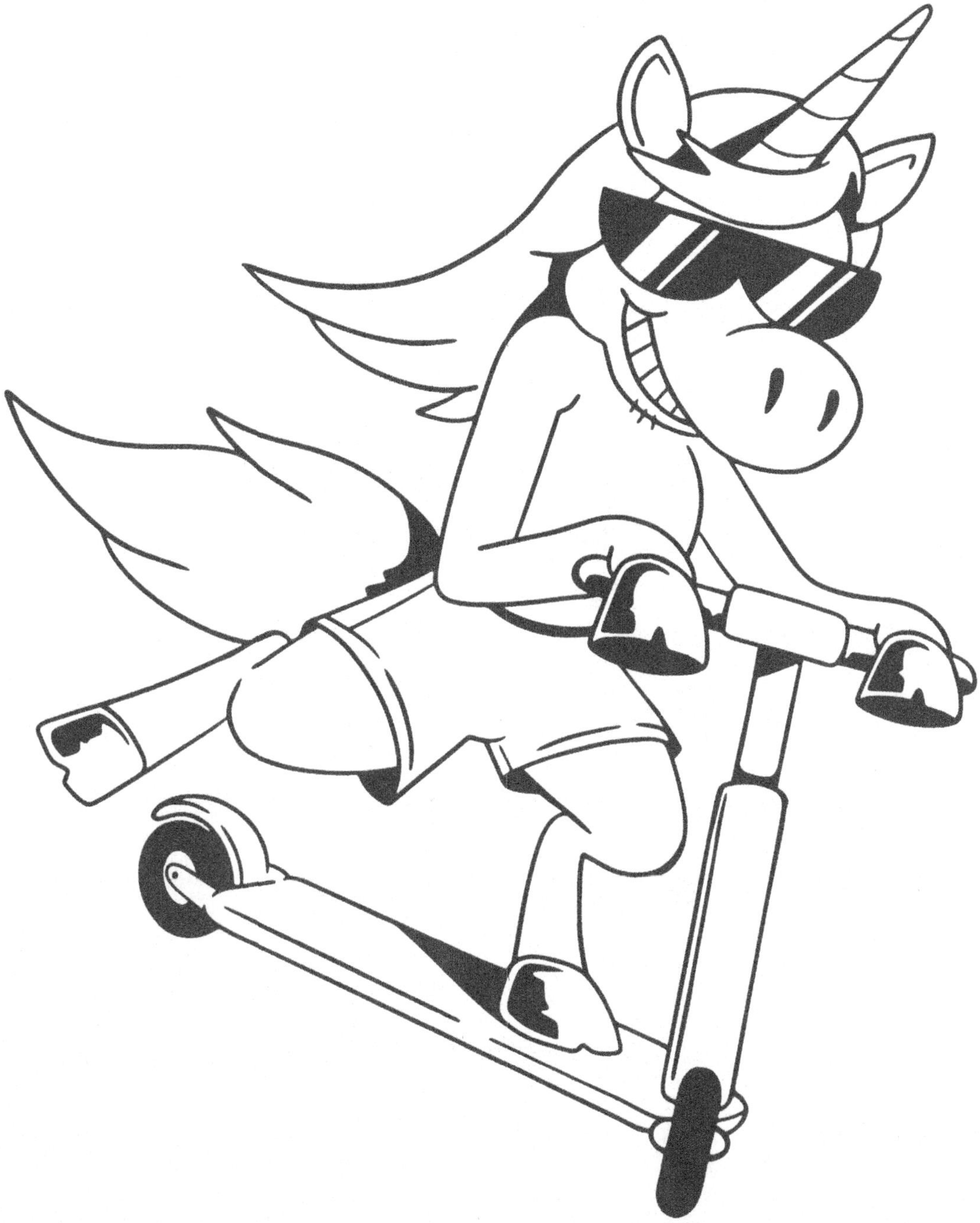

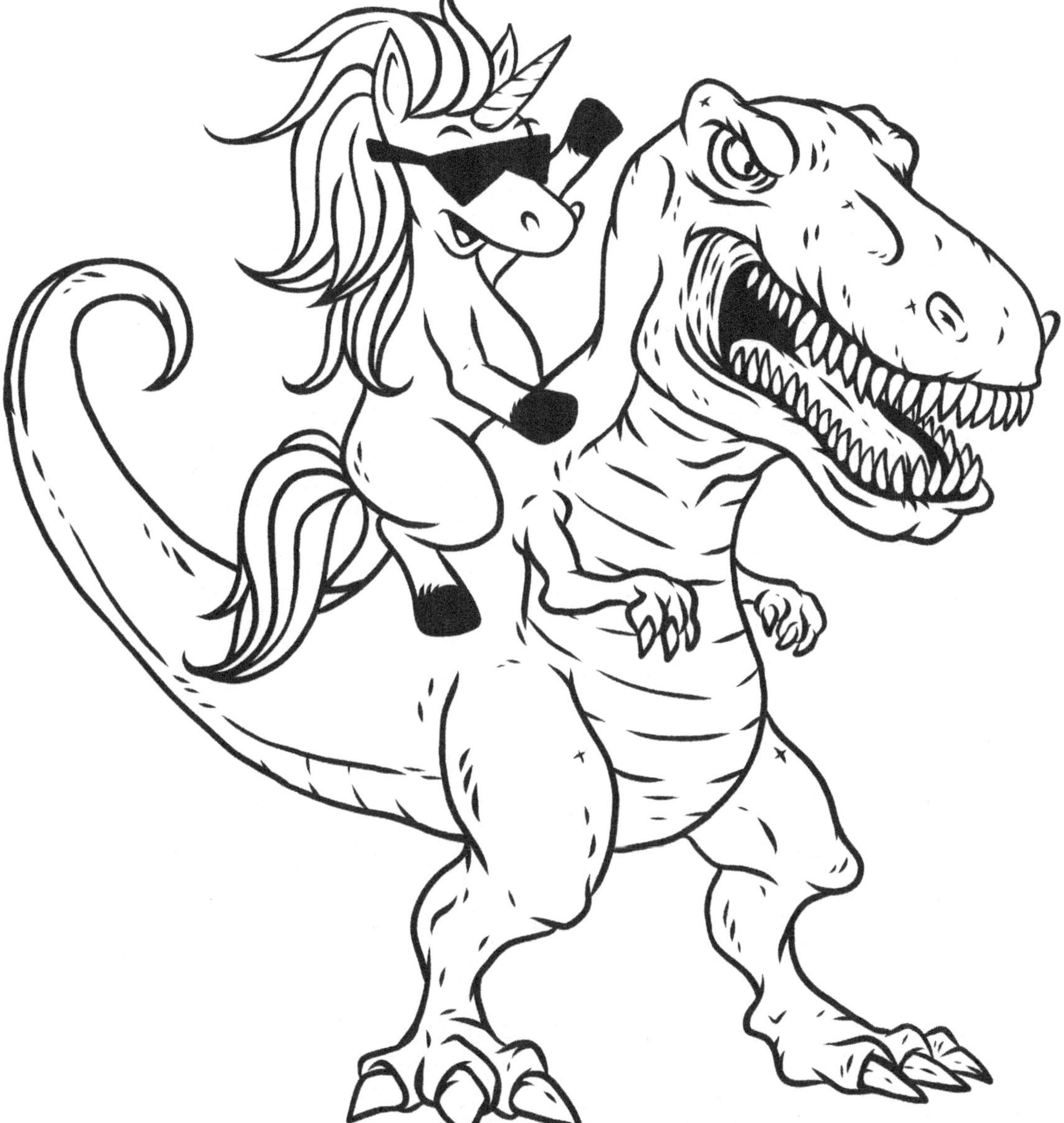

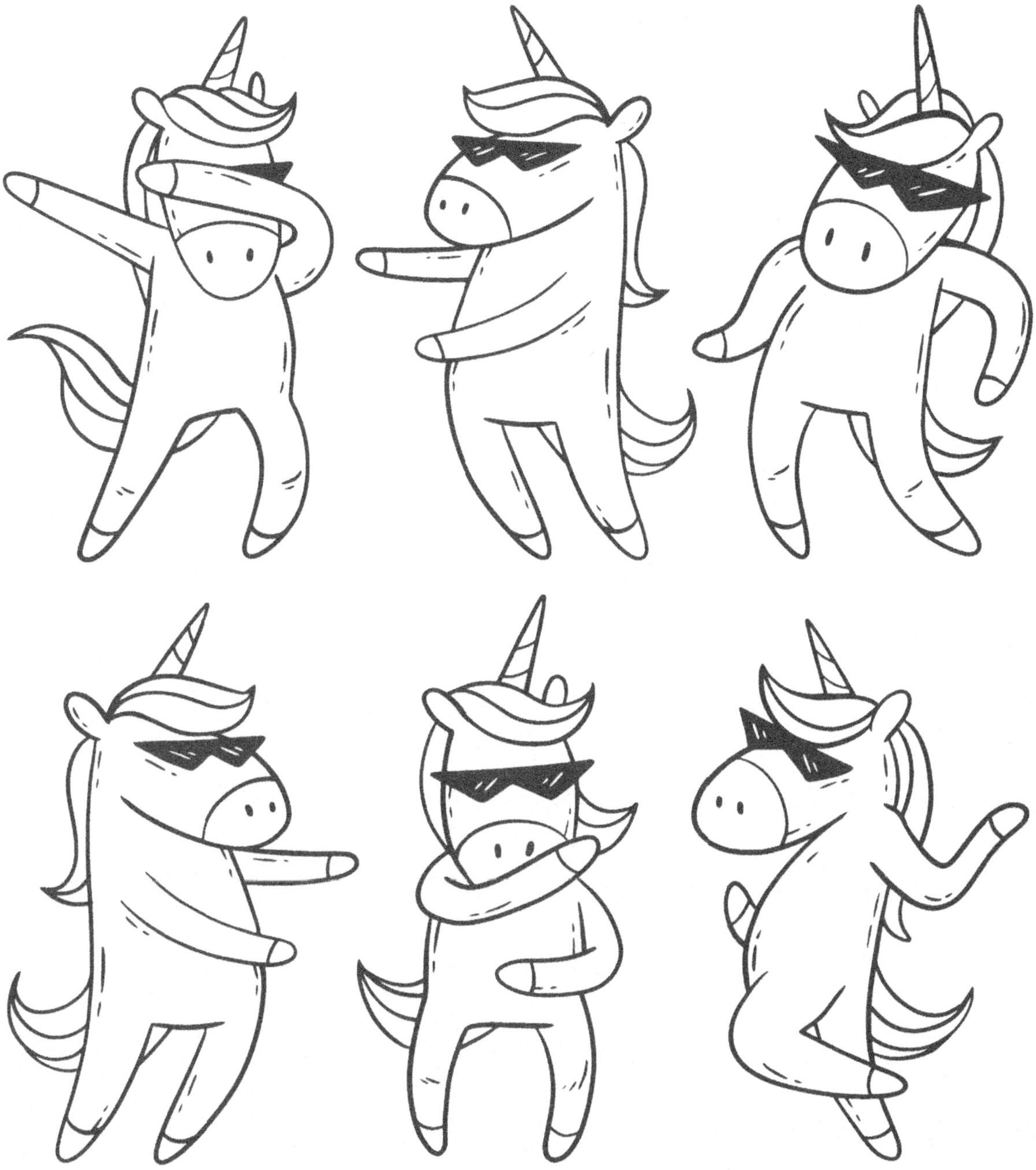

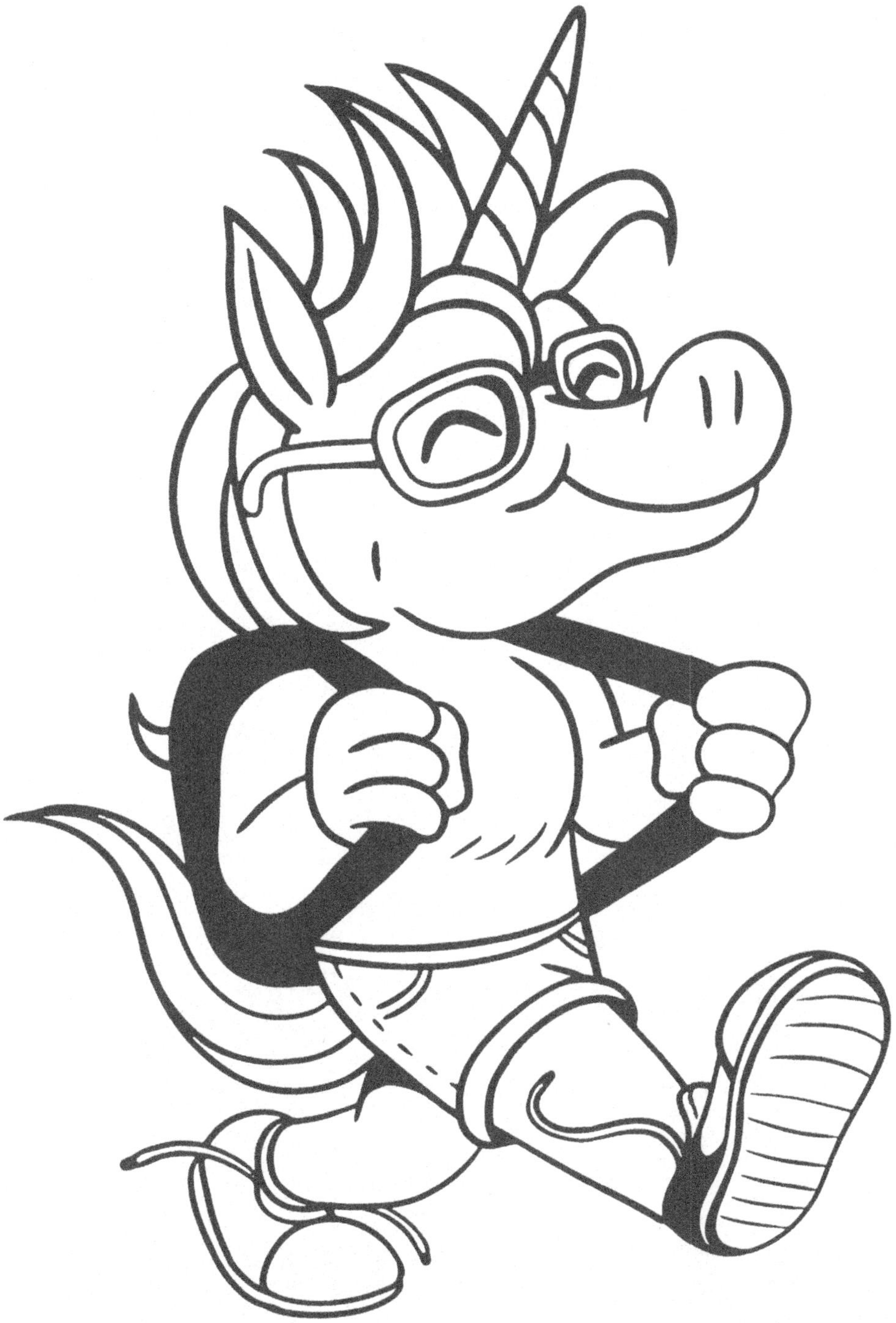

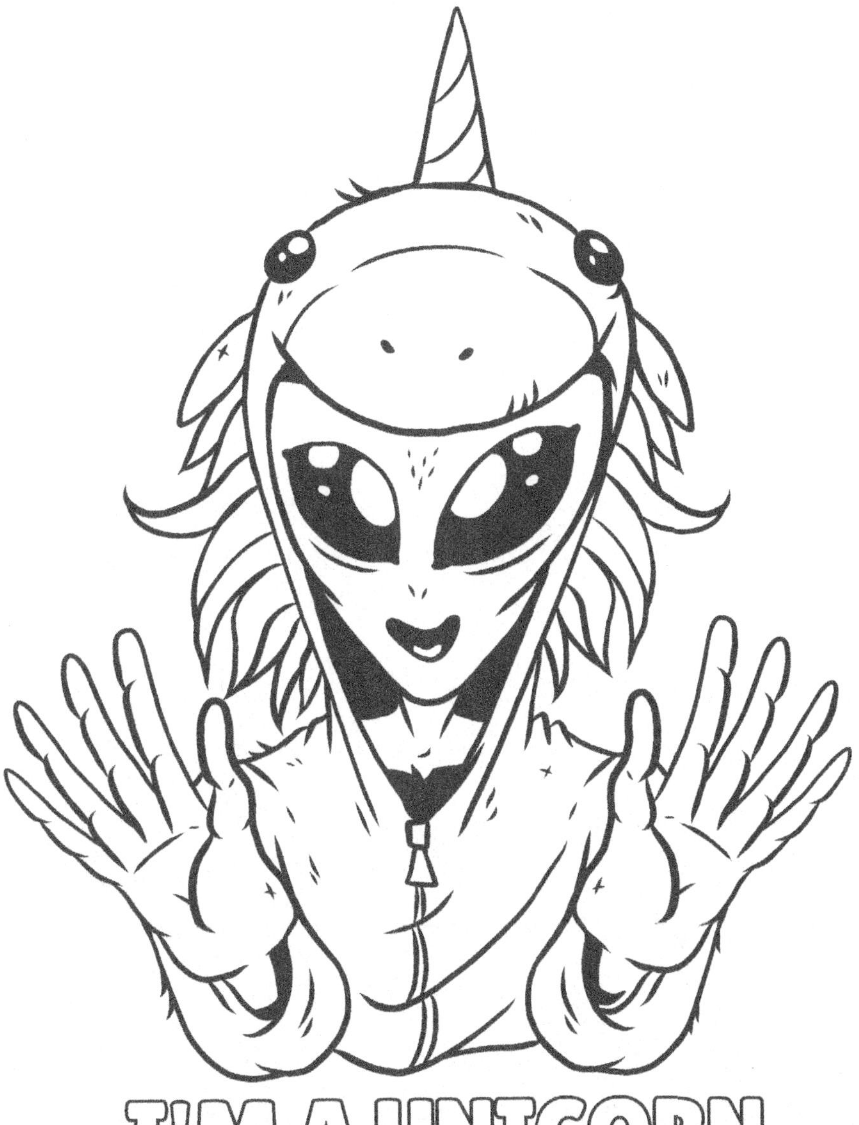

I'M A UNICORN

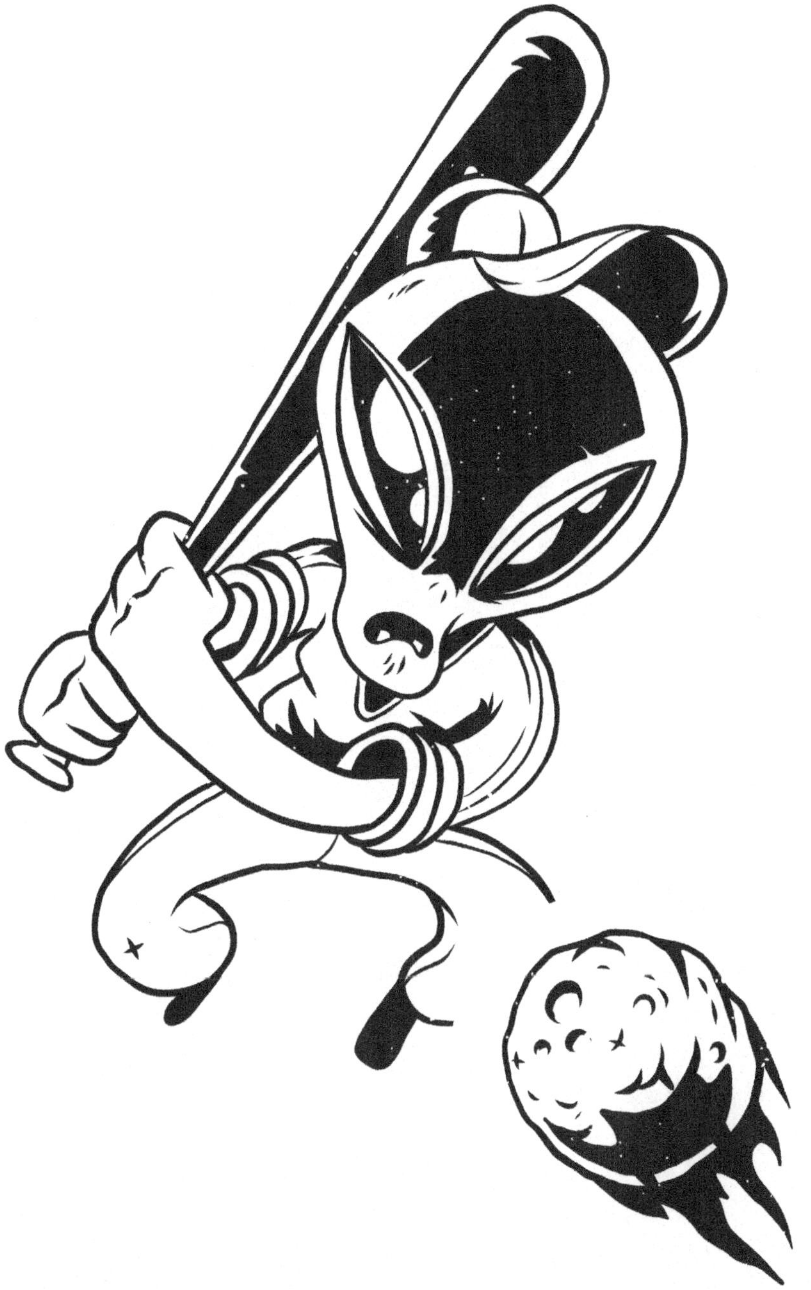

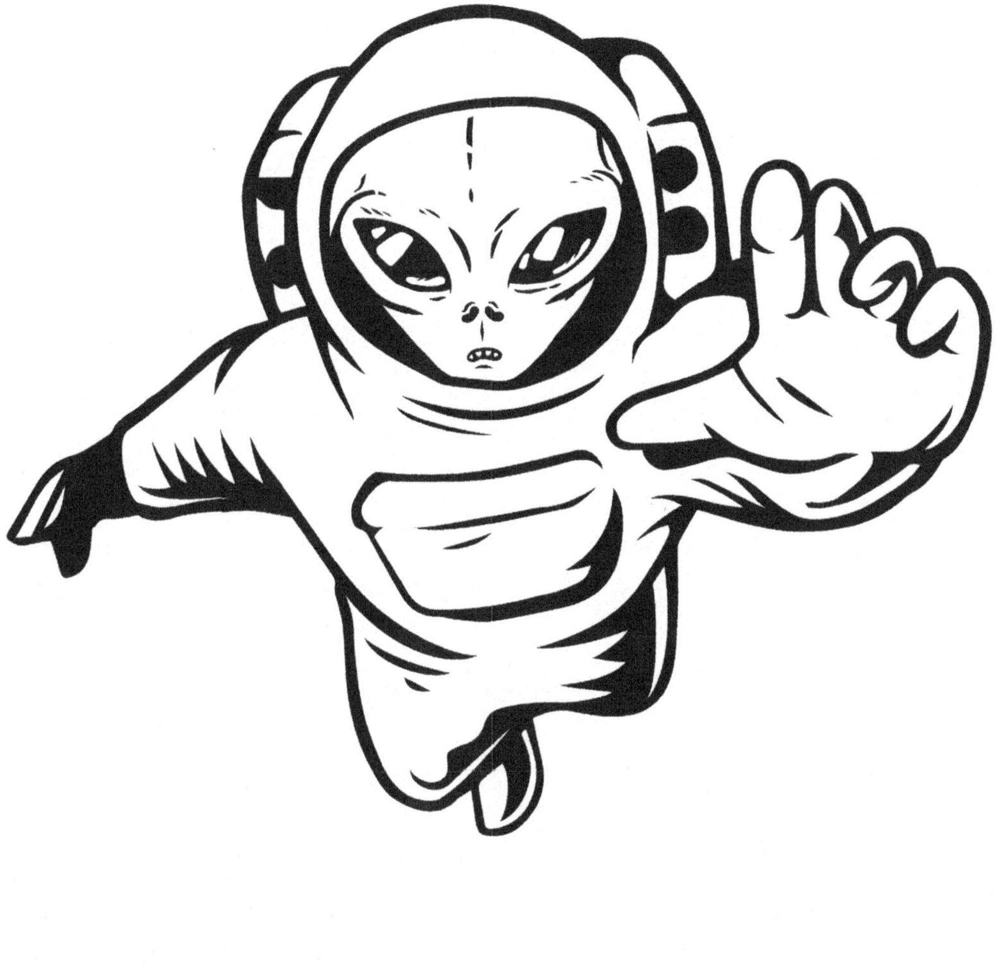

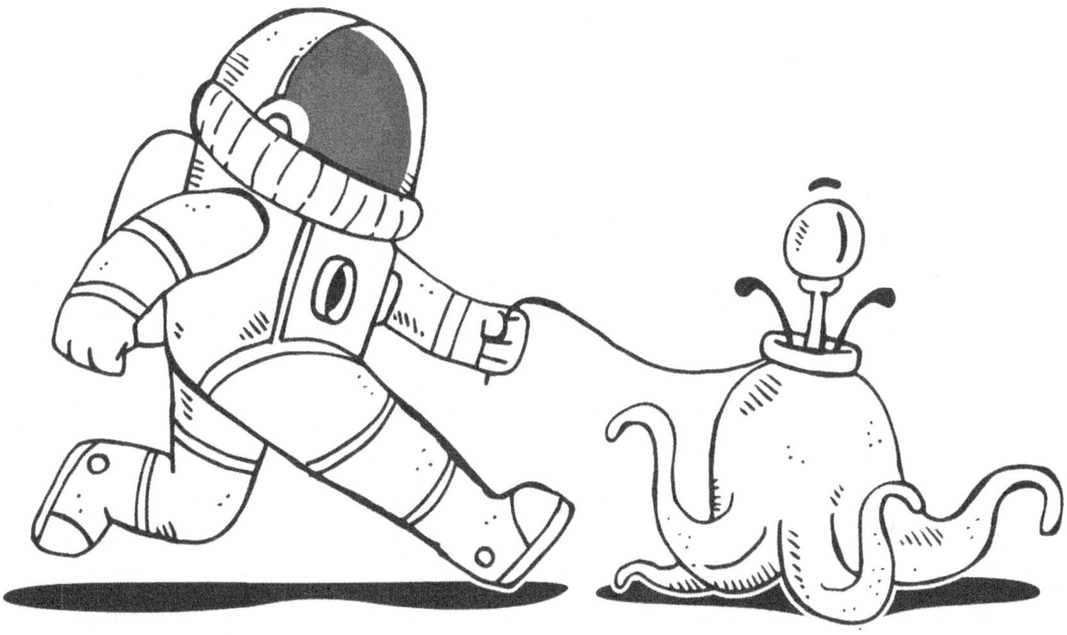

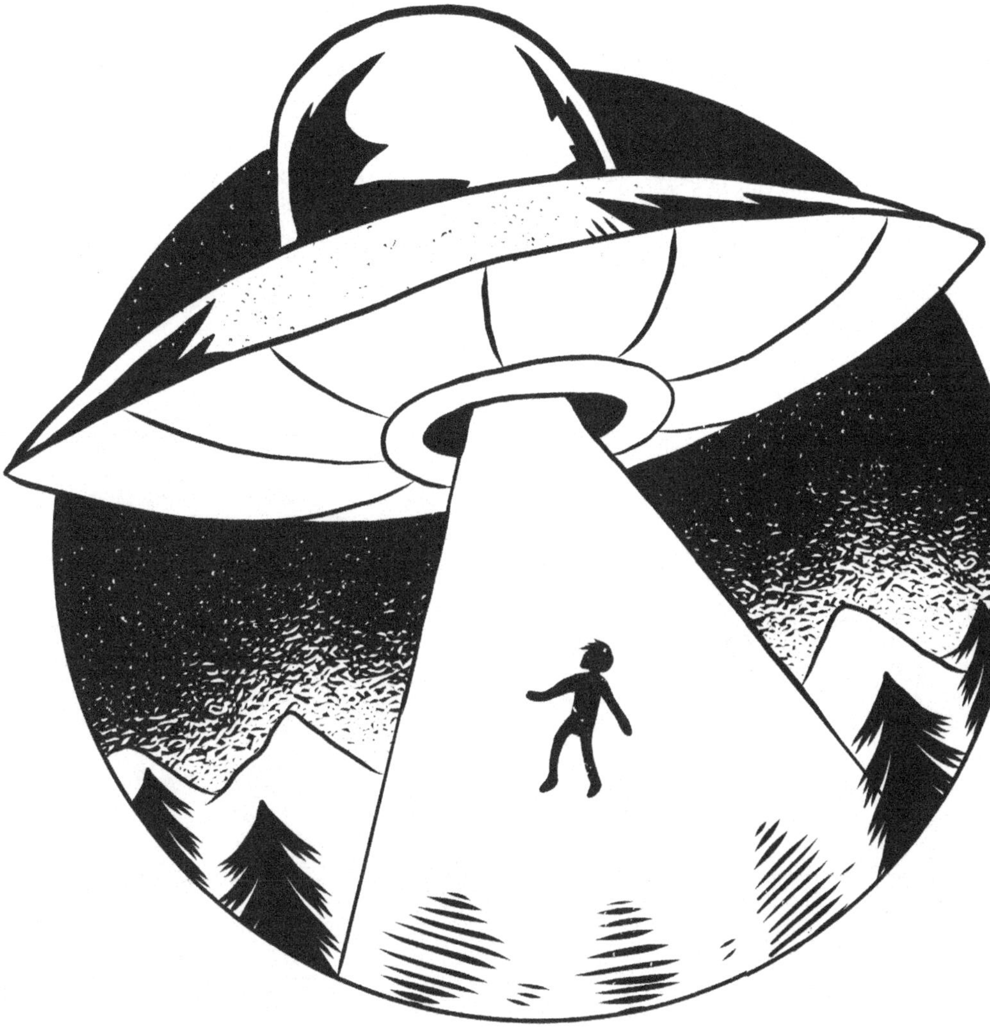

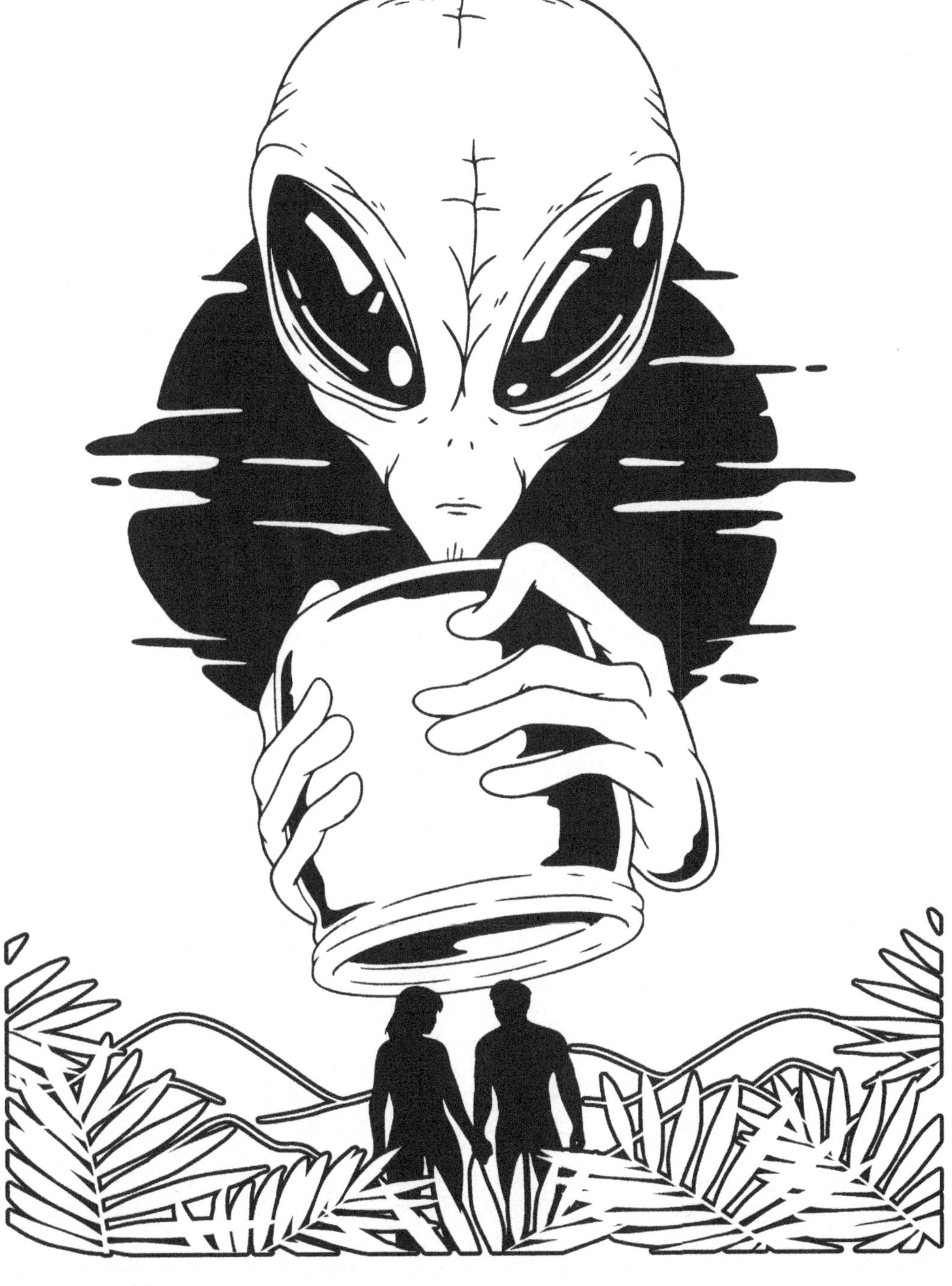

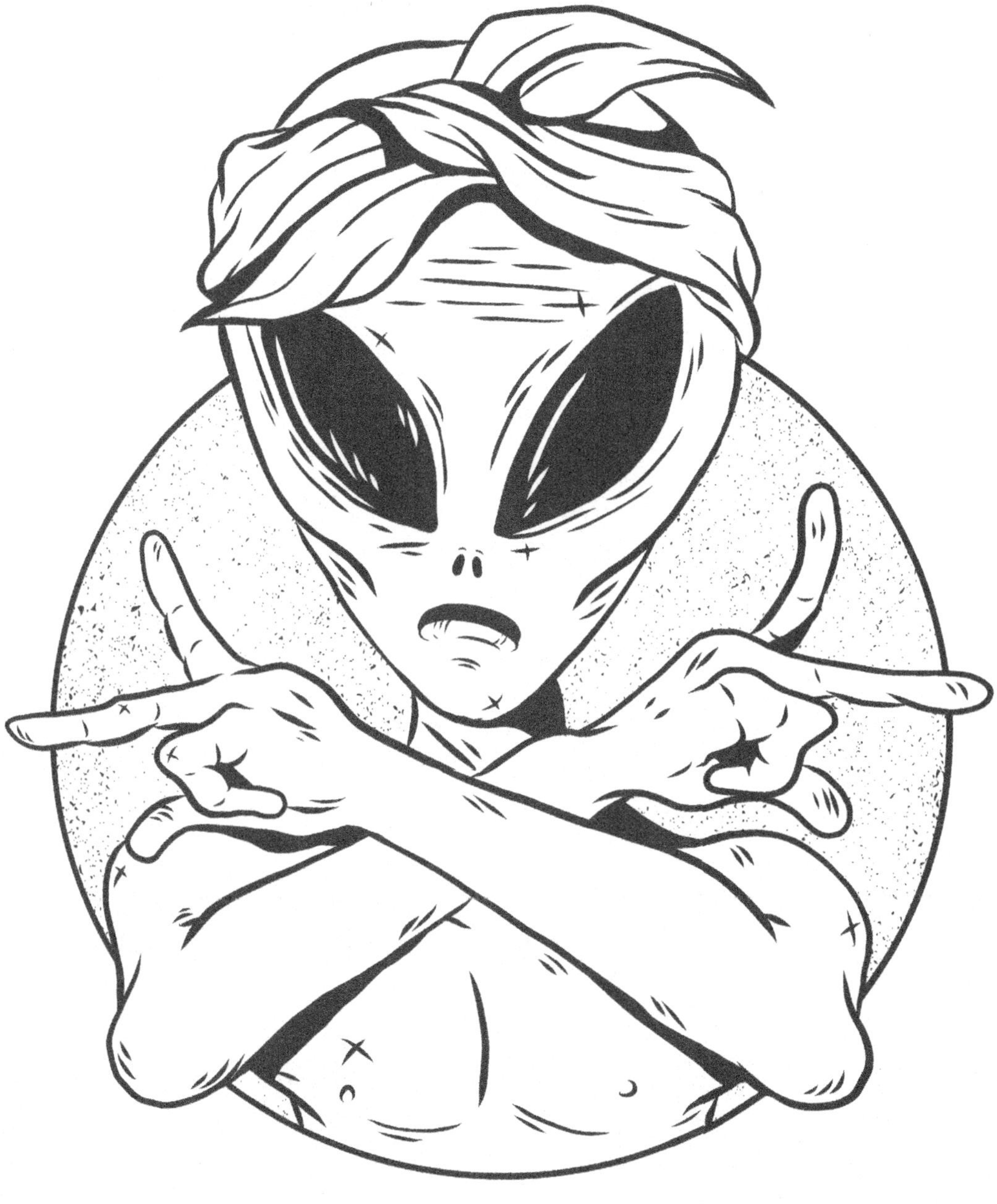

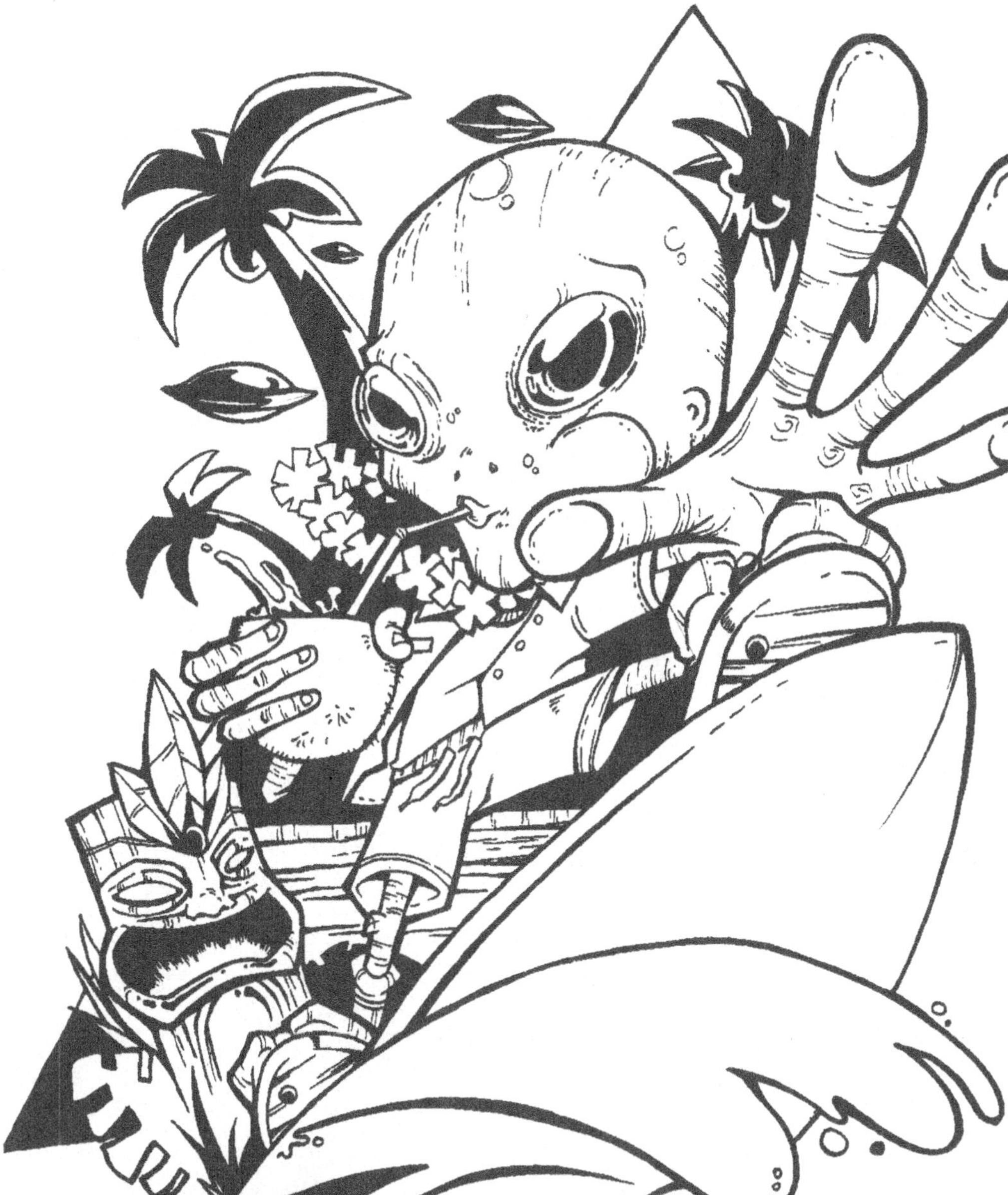

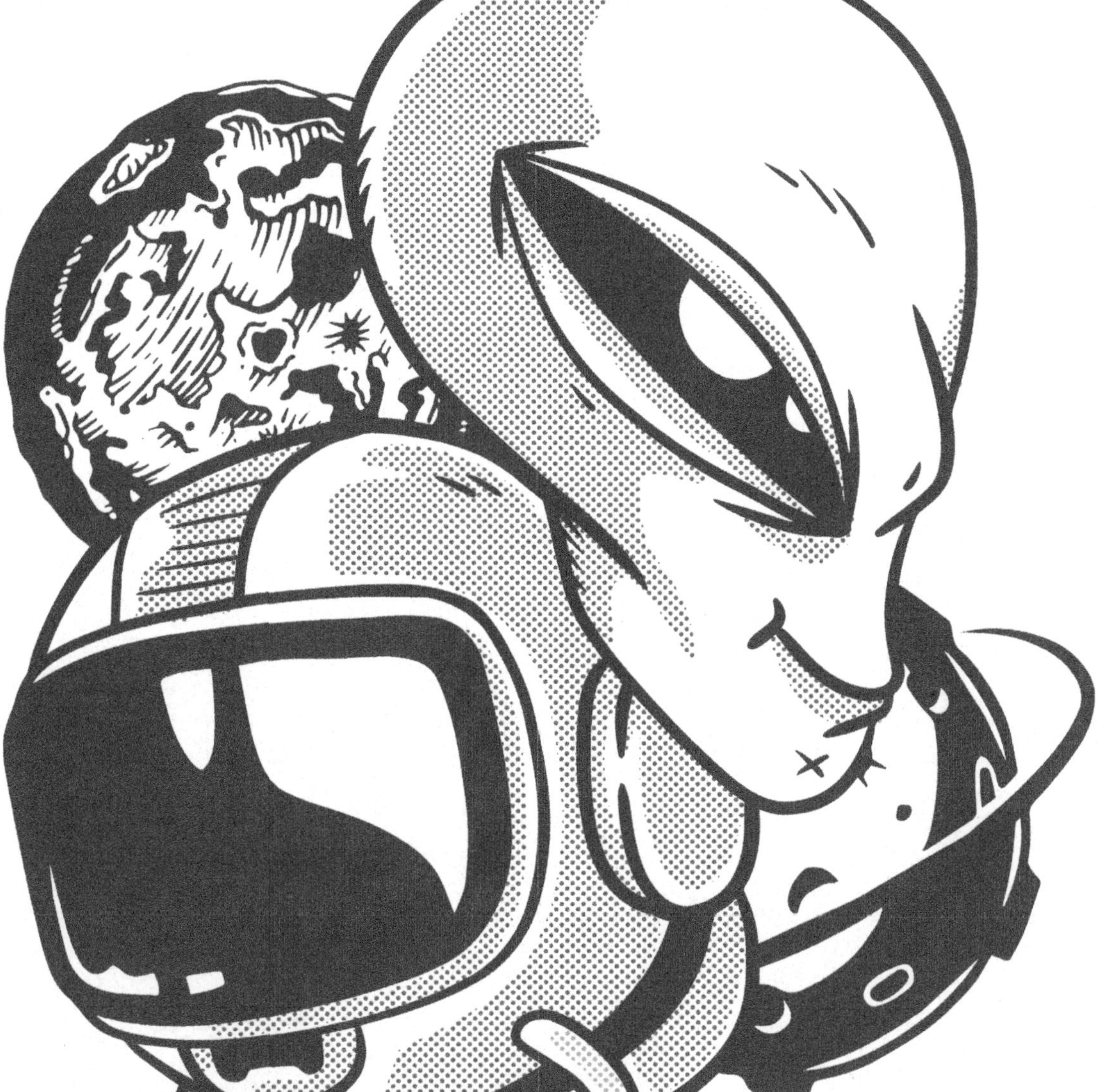

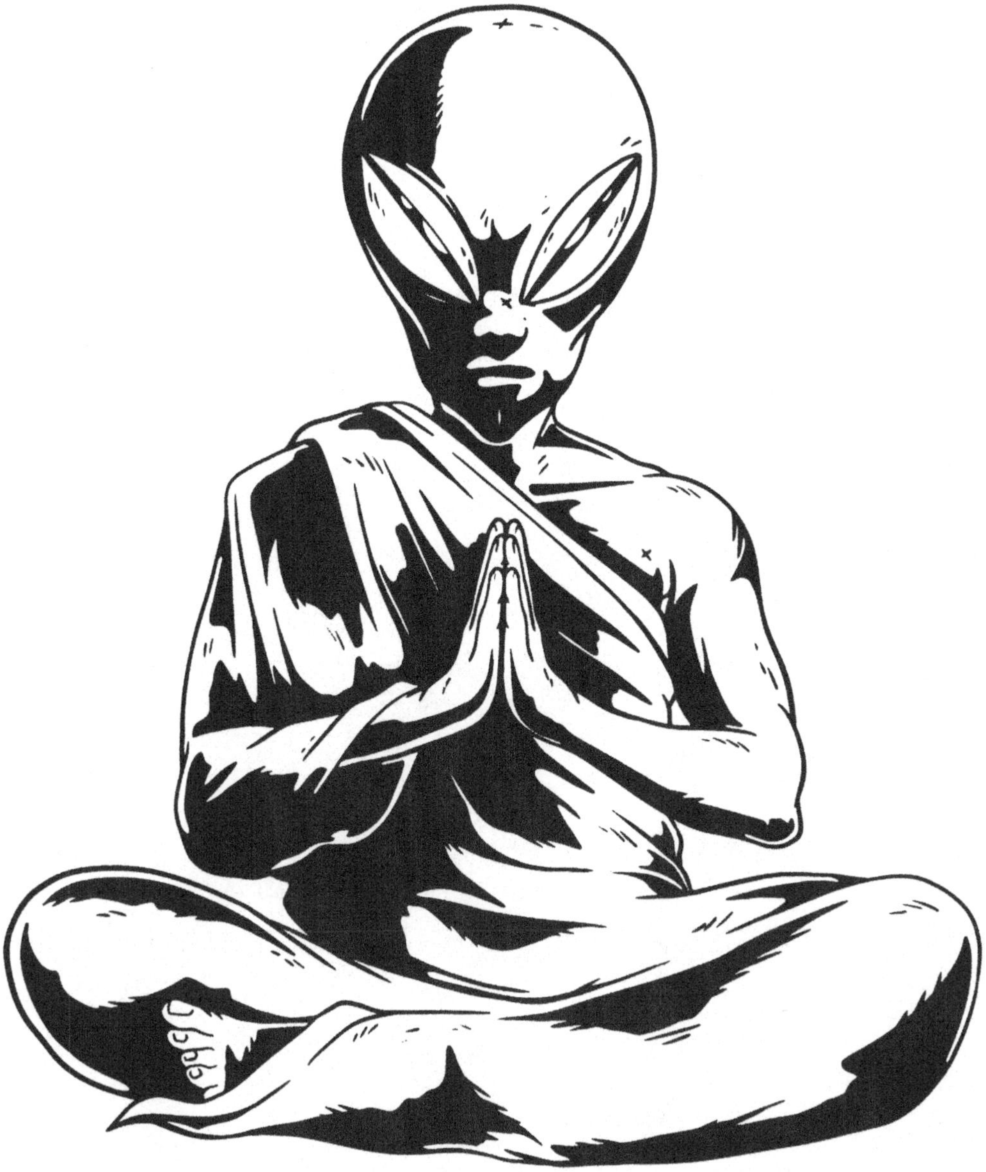

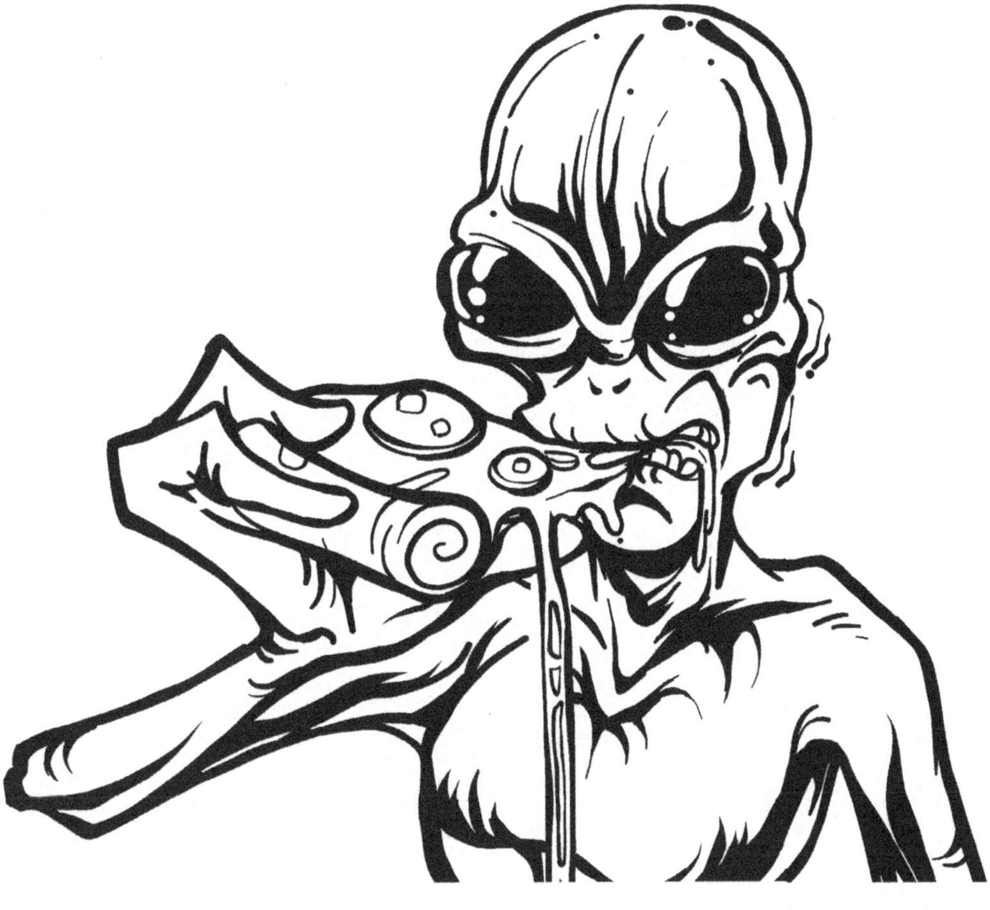

Made in the USA
Columbia, SC
04 December 2024

48437272R00037